POETRY AND PRAYER

This unique and attractively bound book holds a diverse collection of rhyming poetry, with something for everyone. It encompasses humour, nostalgia, romance, and a very evident concern about the pollution of our environment. It looks at the past, present, and future, reminding us that God is omnipresent.

The author has a succinct way of bringing each underlying thought into sharp focus with the last verse or line. This elegant book with its dark green binding and gold block title, will grace any coffee table, and also make an ideal gift.

POETRY AND PRAYER

Patricia Thomas

First published in Great Britain in 1998 by

POPPET BOOKS

3 Lancaster Drive, Broadstone, Dorset.
BH18 9EQ.

First printed in Great Britain, 1998

British Library Cataloguing-in-Publication Data.
A catalogue record for this book is available from the British Library.

ISBN 0 9532243 0 9

Printed in Great Britain by
Arthur H. Stockwell Ltd.
Elms Court Torrs Park Ilfracombe
Devon

ACKNOWLEDGEMENTS

The author wishes to acknowledge the following publishers, who have previously included some of these poems in their anthologies or magazines:— Triumph House, Anchor Books. Arrival Press. International Society of Poets. The Association of Teachers of Speech and Drama.

INTRODUCTION

Hello. This is my first collection of poetry and prayer, which I hope you will enjoy.

Poetry has been a close companion throughout my life, and whenever a deep emotion or special occasion has needed colourful description, then poetry fulfilled that requirement. I believe that it is quite the nicest way of saying things.

Simplicity of verse form has been my policy when selecting poems for this anthology. Many people enjoy poetry that rhymes and scans, and are also pleased when they can relate to thoughts expressed.

I have constantly sought guidance for my work through prayer, and have been blessed with many friends who have given me great encouragement and inspiration.

A donation from the proceeds of this book will be made to Diabetes Research.

Wishing you quiet moments with *Poetry and Prayer*.

Patricia Thomas.

CONTENTS

THREE ASPIRATIONS

If I should aspire to write,
May it be not mean or trite.
Whether poetry or prose,
Let it be of help to those
Whose eye shall fall upon the text,
That they may not be hurt nor vexed.

If I should aspire to paint,
May my efforts never taint.
Thoughts of those who gaze upon
Pictures left when I am gone.
Rather may they prove a treasure,
Giving folk unending pleasure.

If I should aspire to sing
Notes that make the rafters ring.
Be it solo, or in choir,
May it set the heart on fire.
Then falling sweetly on the ear
Shall music soothe, and calm all fear.

If I pray, and then believe,
All these things I can achieve.
With humility and grace
Brighten up this earthly place.
Yet Lord, these aspirations three
Are only possible with Thee.

A PRAYER FOR QUIET MOMENTS

Keep us as we rush,
To work, to school, to town,
Then give us quiet moments
That we may pause, and just sit down.

When we talk to Thee
About our cares and strife,
Show us that we must slow down
To enjoy the fullness of life.

Jesus, You lived here,
And felt the strains and stress,
Then You went to rest and pray
Alone, into the wilderness.

As we seek Thy help,
Needing to pray to Thee,
Grant us Lord, that we may find
A garden of Gethsemane.

THE GIFT

"It's the thought that counts," they chanted,
As I stared in disbelief
At the multi-coloured bedsocks,
And the spotted handkerchief.

The family sat there chuckling,
They continue to deride,
"What thought went into that?" I said,
And just pushed them to one side.

Then later on that Christmas night,
As we ate our festive fare,
I thought again about that gift,
Well meaning, and packed with care.

I went to bed with thankful heart,
And, praying for friends so dear
Concluded, "Please forgive me Lord.
I shall pass it on next year."

MY COUNTRYSIDE OF YESTERYEAR

Around the town where I was born,
The countryside has changed its face.
Where barley grew, and golden corn,
Now crops of houses fill the space.

Down Meadow Lane, and through Crook Stile
Was once a green and pleasant stroll.
A peaceful place to dream awhile,
Until construction took its toll.

In fields along the old main road,
Gymkhanas, fetes, and fairs were held.
Loudspeakers blared, and faces glowed.
Then builders came, and trees were felled.

At Forty Acres by the wheat,
We squeezed through rusty kissing gate,
Then ran to reach the iron seat,
Where now new homes proliferate.

Through Wellhead Lane, by cricket ground,
To Grassy Slope, and fertile wood,
Where pure spring water once was found.
Now bikers ride where hazels stood.

Upon the hills I used to find
Flowers that only grow on chalk.
Now desecrated by mankind
Who ride in cars, and do not walk.

The chalk white horse was always there.
(I used to sit upon its eye).
Now grey, cemented, seems to glare
At belching chimney, too close by.

That ancient horse carved on the hill,
Will oversee the future days.
Yet, musing, I remember still,
When people walked in greener ways.

URCHFONT MANOR

Not for me the crowded beach,
The busy town or tourist trail.
Take me to that haven fair,
That stands within the Pewsey Vale.

Urchfont Manor and estate.
Elizabethan elegance.
Nestling near the mustard fields,
And where the chalk white horses prance.

Crunch on golden gravel drive
Until you reach the big front door.
Step into the spacious hall,
There old oak chest, and flagstone floor.

Join a residential course.
Develop skills, or learn anew.
Lectures in the library.
Conversation, and music too.

Take a walk around the grounds.
Brick walled gardens, wrought iron gates.
Fruit and vegetables grown
Are served up on the dinner plates.

Flower borders, croquet lawn.
Artists paint as you drift along.
All is blessed peacefulness,
Until you hear the meal time gong!

This for me, the tranquil scene.
Not just to rest, but to achieve.
Mind and body are refreshed.
A perfect respite I believe.

THE RIVER WYLE

Watch me wandering, and winding
Lazily through verdant valley.
Slipping by the misty meadows,
Taking time to dilly-dally.

I think about the old main road
That synchronised its way with mine.
Now, a new bypass takes the strain,
Stretching in straight unyielding line.

If, like me, you can meander
From the busy throbbing highways,
You will find the quiet village,
As you travel on the byways.

Visit the sturdy stone built church
That occupies a central place.
Ever the hub of village life,
As God endows us with His grace.

Little shelters hide in hedgerows,
Where people wait to board the bus.
Observing all I wend my way,
And ponder matters aqueous.

My gravel bed is full of silt,
And the stifling weed is growing.
I ask mankind to clear my course,
So that I can keep on flowing.

WAITING

Here we are, waiting again.
Queuing for bus, catching the train.
Sitting in surgery nursing a pain.

Booking in and booking out.
Patient we are without a doubt,
When clinics keep us waiting about.

Shopping can be such a chore
Here at the checkout in the store.
Friendly words make it less of a bore.

Waiting to collect their dues,
Pensioners stand in quiet queues,
With plenty of time to think and muse.

Make good use of waiting time,
Compose a tune, or write a rhyme,
For idle thoughts are such a crime.

"Thoughts are living things" they say,
So use some waiting time each day
To think of others, and then to pray.

DORSET DAYS

Dorset days are golden days,
Sunlit shores and shining bays
Giving life a golden haze.

Dorset days are silver days,
Rivers wind where people laze
Basking in the silver rays.

Dorset days are happy days,
Church and minster sound their lays
Ringing out a happy phrase.

Dorset days are peaceful days,
Quiet walks and tranquil ways
By the sheep that peaceful graze.

Dorset days are thankful days,
Here we live, and here we praise
God, who gave us Dorset days.

BROADSTONE

Still called "The Village",
Though more like a town.
Broadstone in Dorset
Never wears a frown.

Stroll down the Broadway,
Plenty there to see.
Friends meeting, greeting,
Chatting cheerfully.

Walk there in summer,
Or sit by the trees.
Still scent lavender
Wafting on the breeze.

Winters are balmy,
Rarely does it snow.
Sometimes smell the sea
When the mild winds blow.

See the fine detail
On the tapestry.
Telling the story
Of its history.

Still called "The Village",
Yet like a small town.
Broadstone in Dorset
Never lets you down.

THE COFFEE LOUNGE

Are you feeling sad, or lonely?
Do you need a cup that cheers?
Then come into the coffee lounge,
Take a seat, and dry those tears.

At a church along the Broadway
An oasis waits for you.
From ten till noon, the coffee lounge
Serves a drink, and biscuit too.

Smiling ladies wait to greet you,
Sometimes gentlemen as well.
So welcome to the coffee lounge,
Friendly meetings, tales to tell.

Are you tired from all that shopping?
Need to rest those aching feet?
Direct them to the coffee lounge.
You will always find a seat.

Are you feeling bright and happy?
Do you have a joy to share?
Just bring it to the coffee lounge.
God is always listening there.

DORSET DELIGHT

Have you been to Dorset?
Visit while you may.
Perfect English county
For a holiday.

If you come to Dorset,
Beauty waits for you.
Peaceful parks and gardens,
Downs and woodlands too.

When you come to Dorset,
Sail on silver seas.
Walk the rugged clifftops,
Sit upon the quays.

Down in deepest Dorset,
Far from madding sound.
Timeless towns and hamlets
Waiting to be found.

Whilst you are in Dorset,
Minster bells will chime.
Wander quiet byways,
Losing count of time.

As you leave this county
Memories may wane.
Let delight in Dorset
Bring you back again.

THE APPLE

"Catch!" The little boy Herbert said.
An apple landed on my bed.
It glowed with yellow, red, and green,
More luscious fruit I had not seen.

As patients in the children's ward,
We both were feeling rather bored.
He could not walk with foot encased.
I, life with diabetes faced.

My future they could not predict,
And diet rules were very strict.
Yet, though it was not time to feed,
I scoffed that apple with great speed.

Nurse came along, and found the core,
Then said, "Do not eat any more."
Uncle Mac, the dietician,
Gave a fearsome admonition.

"Diet rules you must ***not*** forget,
You don't want to see Jesus yet."
How could he not appreciate
That I was just a child aged eight?

That happened many years ago,
And times have changed, thankfully so.
Poor Uncle Mac would be surprised
That diets now have been revised.

I live my life the healthy way,
Eat an apple every day.
And still I am not in my box.
How strange, that boy's surname was Cox!

RENEWAL

We thank You God for the seasons,
And the contrasts that they bring.
For the warmth of summer sunshine,
Then the autumn harvesting.
For winter days of frost and snow
Now mellowing into spring.

Nature is once again renewed.
Life from cold earth is springing.
Hope blossoms in the human heart,
It is a new beginning,
And, thus restored we journey on,
Your praises ever singing.

SPRINGTIME WITH GILBERT AND SULLIVAN

"We know that spring is on the way"
The people of the town would say
On hearing talk of G. and S.
"Which one this year? Now, let me guess."

Music, drama, we loved it all.
From January, at the hall.
Rehearsals would be underway
Until the show in early May.

Produced since nineteen-forty-one.
Proudly presented, and well done.
Church tradition at Monkton Hill
Has endured, and flourishes still.

For many years I sang along,
Feeling privileged to belong
To such a happy friendly group,
A talented and intrepid troupe.

It brought fresh purpose to my life,
At times when I knew pain and strife.
So now, when starting to spring-clean,
I hear those tunes so evergreen.

THE SPRINGTIME KISS

Through all the seasons of the year
I admired you constantly.
Yet the words remained unspoken,
For this love could never be.

Your life and mine so different
That our paths would never meet.
You were gentle, charismatic,
Professionally elite.

Then one May morn we met by chance
In a quiet wooded chine.
We walked, and talked of many things.
I adored your voice divine.

Here, at last we stood together,
Your eyes burned deep into mine.
Nothing could separate us now
As I touched your face so fine.

You drew me so close, and held me
Then our lips met in a kiss.
I wished it would last for ever,
For nothing had been like this.

My heart was now pounding wildly,
More than real it all did seem.
But suddenly then, I woke up!
It was a ***lovely*** dream.

SUMMER THANKSGIVING

For summer flowers,
And shady bowers,
Refreshing showers,
We thank You, Lord.

For the bird songs sweet,
And fresh fruits to eat,
Those dear friends to meet,
We thank You, Lord.

For warm balmy days
Spent in quiet ways,
Psalms and hymns of praise,
We thank You, Lord.

For all joy and mirth
Shared upon this earth,
Then for our own birth
We thank You, Lord.

SUMMER SONNET

Mellow yellow is the city of Bath,
Warmly glowing in the summer sunshine.
Descend on busy road or hillside path
Into that all-embracing spa so fine.
There, circus and crescent curve and caress,
And leafy squares provide a cooling shade.
Stroll through floral byways, where people press
To hear the violin and flute well played.
See Pulteney Bridge, and River Avon Weir,
Then on to where the stately abbey stands
With Roman Baths and Pump Rooms nestling near.
The visitors still come from many lands,
For Aquae Sulis I shall always yearn.
To the city of Bath I ***must*** return.

THE FIVE SENSES

Seeing faces of friends, and loved ones so dear.
Great glories of nature around me all year.
Theatrical shows, colours, drama and dance.
Books, beauty and paintings that doth life enhance.

Melodious music, composed by the great.
Much good conversation, with tales to relate.
Mellifluous voices that float on the air.
Clear birdsong, and laughter that banishes care.

Aromas recalling those times from the past,
And delicate perfumes that linger and last.
That freshly baked bread leading me to the shop.
Those coffee beans roasting, I just have to stop!

The exquisite flavours of food when I dine,
Accompanied by that most excellent wine.
The chocolate mousse that I just could not miss,
And sweet lips of one that I most like to kiss.

Stroking the foliage of herbs, shrubs and trees,
And playing sweet music on piano keys.
Caressing the sculpture, its curve, line, or sphere,
Then holding the one that I love very near.

POETRY AND PRAYER

Poetry helps us
Express what we feel.
Those well chosen lines
Convey and reveal.

Poetry lifts us
From depths of despair.
Poetry comforts,
When written to share.

Life is a poem
From first to last breath.
Love is a poem
From birth until death.

A reason for rhyme
Is readily found.
And reasons for prayer?
Well, just look around.

BUTTERFLY

A butterfly with injured wing,
Is in the garden fluttering,
Striving to alight the flower,
Hungry, weak, from loss of power.

Then let me lift you little friend,
Upon my finger now ascend.
Feed on the nectar, till at length
You will have quite regained your strength.

So butterfly with injured wing
Rests on flower, recovering,
And soon it flutters, then it flies
Away into the summer skies.

THE SEA

By day and night, in dark and light,
I'm always by the sea.
It fills my dreams, in them it seems
I'm ever by the sea.

I climb the rocks and tour the docks,
It's always by the sea.
The lighthouse beams pervade my schemes.
Again, I'm by the sea.

I've seen it rough, when life is tough
For people by the sea.
But when it's calm, the healing balm
Flows freely from the sea.

Now every day my thoughts just stray
To a home that's by the sea.
A haven fair, I know not where,
But it must be by the sea.

I'll pass my days in many ways,
So happy by the sea.
And when I die I hope to lie
So peaceful by the sea.

AUNTIE AMY

Auntie Amy is eighty-eight,
Yet, there she is out by the gate
Still braving wind and rain, or snow,
To wave to folk as home they go.

Our Auntie Amy sits and knits
Warm woolly jumpers, socks and mitts.
All presents for her family
To place around the Christmas tree.

Auntie Amy will often sing
Praises to our Heavenly King.
Hymns and verses, chorus and song,
She teaches as we sing along.

And Auntie Amy always prays
To God, who orders all her days.
She visits those who need her there
To share a trouble, grief, or care.

Auntie Amy has come to stay,
Now we are happy every day.
For peace, and love, and joy abound
When Auntie Amy is around.

DISCIPLINE

Discipline is lacking now
In many walks of life.
Each person wants their freedom,
Thus, causing others strife.

Self-discipline is needed,
We should not be self-willed.
Respect for all around us
Be constantly instilled.

Citizenship, a concept
That must be held by all.
Concern for other people,
Assistance when they fall.

Deterrents too, are failing
To fight the drugs and crime.
Why should our older people
Feel threatened all the time?

Discipline is a harsh word,
And must go hand in hand
With love and understanding,
For peace throughout the land.

MISUNDERSTOOD

Lord, when I am wrongly blamed
For things I did not do.
When others set themselves up
As judge, and jury too,
And cease communication.
I still can talk to You.

Lord, when You were sent to die,
And hung upon the cross,
You did not blame another
In this world full of dross.
You simply bore our burdens,
And did not count Your loss.

TRUE FRIENDS

Imagine life without friends
In whom we can confide.
Those very special people
Who always care and guide.

Friends that we have known for years
Accept us as we are.
They have that understanding,
If they are near or far.

Such friendships must be nurtured.
Be sure to keep in touch.
Giving of your time to them,
But not taking too much.

True friends will always listen,
Not judge, nor criticise.
They never are self-righteous,
Though sometimes can advise.

Acquaintances are many.
True friends are, but a few.
Yet, our greatest friend is God,
For He is ever true.

SCENES OF LIFE

Life is full of ups and downs,
Of goings in and out.
Some sunny smiles, and frequent frowns,
Belief, yet often doubt.

We all must feel both joy and pain
Throughout our earthly life.
To welcome sunshine after rain,
And calm that follows strife.

We ought to be both rich and poor
To taste the sweet and sour.
And people who have lived through war
Embrace the peaceful hour.

In life we learn to love or hate,
Making heaven or hell.
God knows our changing scenes of life.
His son came here to dwell.

A LETTER TO THE QUEEN
(Celebrating Her Majesty's 70th Birthday)

Dear Ma'am. Congratulations, in this your special year.
I am sending salutations, heartfelt, and most sincere.
On your day of coronation, those solemn vows you gave,
Setting the finest example of how we should behave.

The worries with your family have brought you many tears.
Be comforted your Majesty, we all have had bad years.
You still have a loving mother to guide you through the days,
And individual children, with very special ways.

Charles cares for the environment, helps cities with Trust grants.
We should all live close to nature. I often talk to plants!
Anne, a daughter to be proud of, dignified and royal.
Helps to save the poorer children. Always very loyal.

Andrew, a dashing naval man, who fought for land and Queen.
A sensitive and caring soul. Quite skilled upon the green.
Edward, a champion of the arts, your gentle youngest son.
With husband, Philip by your side, life must sometimes be fun.

And, Ma'am, you keep your promises, for better or for worse,
So that is why I am inspired, to pen this humble verse.
In conclusion, may I venture to ask you if I can,
Why does the Poet Laureate still have to be a man?

THE ART GALLERY

Skylight windows, and wood block floors.
Art assembled, with guard by doors.
Picture lighting on warm washed walls,
Gives ambience throughout the halls.

Leather seating in central place
Lends perspective with time and space.
Artistic skills displayed, to show
Title and name on plaque below.

Paintings hanging, sculptures posing.
People pointing, old folk dozing.
Foreheads frowning, heads inclining.
What can ***that*** be? Nude reclining!

Footsteps echo on the flooring.
Guard now resting, gently snoring.
Find the tearoom, souvenir shop.
Feeling weary, so have to stop.

Coffee or tea, and milky shakes.
Thin sandwiches and sticky cakes.
A peaceful place, I think I may
Return again another day.

SEA MUSIC

Listen to the symphony,
Hear the sea music play,
As swelling waves crescendo,
Then break, and fade away.

The surging surf suffuses
My sad, sorrowing soul.
Soothing, calming, and healing,
Until I am made whole.

MY MUSIC TEACHER

She nurtured my love of good music
In manner so genteel and mild,
And taught me to play the piano,
When I was still only a child.

She sat by my side with a notebook,
Commanding the utmost respect.
I perched on the stool, loosened my wrists,
Made sure that my back was erect.

She taught me to sing, training my voice,
And then as my confidence grew,
Entered me for the eisteddfod,
Thus setting the challenges new.

A truly professional lady,
Who also conducted the choir.
Her love and devotion to music,
Was something for all to admire.

She cared for each one of her pupils,
And standards were set very high.
Memories of her are immortal,
For someone like that doesn't die.

A modest, yet talented lady,
Whose name you might well try to guess.
At the close of each music lesson
She would simply sign E M S.

THE CARER'S PRAYER

Help me Lord from day to day,
As I care for one so dear.
May I be always cheerful,
And hide any selfish tear.

Lord, support me week by week,
As I strive to do my best.
Grant me health and strength to cope,
And recharge me when I rest.

Lord, stay close, as month by month
I travel on this highway.
Banish all resentful thoughts,
For I must do it Thy way.

Give me grace from year to year
To find that joy in serving.
Let my faith and caring be
Devoted and unswerving.

BEYOND MORTALITY

In my younger days, I used to find
That, having a most enquiring mind,
I searched for truths of spiritual kind.

So thus, with great anticipation
Joined in circles of meditation,
And even witnessed levitation.

Went to meetings to hear clairvoyants,
Yet, sometimes found to my annoyance
How skilled they were at truth avoidance.

Though when at sanctuaries kneeling,
I knew that warm celestial feeling
Of peace, that comes with spirit healing.

I have been so privileged to see
Spirit life beyond mortality,
And for this I offer thanks to Thee.

Now older, wiser, longer in tooth,
I have no need to search for the truth.
Faith has grown since the days of my youth.

NOVEMBER

November is the month I hate,
So full of dark and dismal fate,
And ushered in by Hallowe'en
When pagan rituals are seen.

The days are foggy, damp, and short,
With fireworks making loud report;
And bonfires smoking everywhere,
Pollute the fresh autumnal air.

Untidiness is all around
As leaves come tumbling to the ground.
The year is dying. It is late.
I wish that I could hibernate.

Remembrance time is also here.
The poppies fall, and bitter tear.
Oh sad November quickly run,
Until your thirty days are done.

UNSEEN GIFTS

Teach us Lord, to value
The gifts we do not see.
Happiness, contentment,
Patience, humility.

Teach us Lord, to cherish
Friendship and constancy.
Kindness and compassion,
Fairness and honesty.

Teach us Lord, to treasure
Blessings divine and free.
All these unseen gemstones
Are precious gifts from Thee.

Teach us Lord, to hold dear
All that is pure and true,
As we journey onwards
Becoming more like You.

PARTY PANIC

I am not a party person,
Much more like a recluse.
When given an invitation
I think of an excuse.

I would have to wear a posh frock,
With high heeled fashion shoes,
And strive to look so elegant,
Then flatter and amuse.

I will not engage in small talk,
Chitchat to everyone.
A meaningful conversation
Is my idea of fun.

The food will be too fattening,
The wine will be too sweet,
And the people will be boring,
Some swaying on their feet.

What is that you say? A soirée,
And ***he*** just might be there.
Well, that's a different matter.
Now, which dress shall I wear?

EXTREME ELEMENTS

A large Atlantic low is looming
Somewhere out in the West.
A howling hurricane is heading
This way, at God's behest.

In the Far East, monsoons are breaking,
Ordained by God's own hand.
The rainy season now pervades,
And water floods the land.

Lascivious lava issues forth.
Volcano now erupts
With rivers of fire and molten rock.
Until God interrupts.

Fear not, yet respect the elements.
We all are born of earth.
Inextricably bound to nature,
We praise God for our birth.

NATURE

God created the world
So beautiful and pure,
Then blessed it with life forms
That we see as nature.
In this wonderful world
That is our planet earth,
We are part of nature,
And give thanks for our birth.

Yet, still we despoil it
In our own foolish ways,
Polluting surroundings
With chemicals and sprays.
With nuclear power
And its radiation,
There is always the risk
Of a conflagration.

Nature may recover,
But we should take more care,
As one day, what is now
Will no longer be there.
Do not oppose nature,
Live close with it instead,
If we do not listen,
We soon shall all be dead.

LAMENT FOR NATURE LOST

Fungicides, insecticides,
Chemicals and pesticides
Spoiling food, polluting air.
Stop it ***now***. Does no-one care?
Fume-filled towns, and acid rain
Causing death and endless pain.

Weed and algae silent creep.
Fertilisers drain and seep
Into the water courses
Poisoning drinking sources.
Bombs, tests, contamination
Spread fears of conflagration.

Selfishness, stupidity,
Avarice and vanity,
Weaknesses of common man,
Not a part of God's great plan.
If we want to live and learn,
Back to nature we must turn.

FUTURE HOPES

There are no dividing lines ’twixt future, present and past.
Future soon becomes today, and the present does not last.
The past leaves us with memories from which we live and learn,
So that future generations may take a wiser turn.
Hopes that everyone accepts the futility of war.
Live, and let all others live, bringing peace for evermore.

History repeats itself for many diverse reasons.
Nothing really changes here, but comes and goes like seasons.
Yet now, we see and know that technology increases.
We also hope that there will be a cure for all diseases.
Mankind will be more healthy, and the life span be increased,
With many more years of leisure, until one is deceased.

Provision for the old folk must extensively improve.
Public transport, meals on wheels, to keep them all on the move!
Each one will have a “Lap-top” so that when they cease to roam,
Goods then ordered from the chair, are delivered to the home.
We can only imagine how the future days might be,
And maybe there are some things that we would not wish to see.

PRAYER FOR THE NEW MILLENNIUM

Lord, may the new millennium
Be happier for mankind.
Mistakes that were made in this one
Be noted, then left behind.

Let knowledge and technology
Be used for the greater good,
So that all existing problems
Can be solved, or understood.

May modern medical research
Be funded and supported,
And good facilities ensure
That progress is not thwarted.

Grant that all the homeless people
Find a place to call their own,
Then, friends with whom to care and share,
For they should not be alone.

Law and order must be restored.
It is very plain to see,
When each one does just as he wants,
Then nobody can be free.

Help us to care for the planet,
Protect our environment.
Restricting use of chemicals
Making nature prevalent.

Let all the nations acknowledge
The futility of war,
Accepting that there is one God
Wanting peace for evermore.

Ring in the new millennium,
And celebrate modestly.
We pray, that future years will bring
Happy days, and unity.